SELF-WORTH

By C J Kruse

INTRODUCTION

Not long ago, I was talking to my counselor. We were discussing the current events in my life, when out of the blue, he asked me a surprising question. He said, "Caleb, can you tell me a few things that you like about yourself?"

Feeling a bit caught off-guard, and not wanting to let it show, I quickly thought of a few of my positive traits and strengths and rattled them off confidently. It sounded something like this; "Well, I'm a good writer, a good musician, and a really nice guy."

My counselor smiled and seemed satisfied by my answers. I however, was not. I wasn't sure if I believed what I had said, or if I had only said it because I knew it was what he wanted to hear. Deep down, a question had been planted. Did I really not know if I was likable?

This simple question lingered in the back of my mind. I felt frustrated by how hard it was to answer. Each time I tried to objectively look at myself, the only thing I could see was my faults and failures. For whatever reason, my positive traits and qualities did not seem as real or as well-defined.

I searched the Scriptures for good things to believe about myself. I began to write down every personal strength and positive trait I possessed, and kept the list nearby in case any moments of self-questioning might arise. I even tried looking in the mirror and speaking these good truths over myself, but none of it helped. In the end, still only my negative traits seemed believable. Why was this? I had to find the answer.

I began to realize that I was on some type of quest, and that it was actually a quest I had been on my whole life – the quest to know my own value. To actually believe in it. To feel sure that I matter, that I have a purpose, and that there's more to me than I've felt. More to me than the world has given me credit for.

Perhaps you know which quest I'm speaking of. You too have been trying to find believable answers to these same questions. If so, then welcome to *The Power Of Self-Worth* – a book about rediscovering our intrinsic value and learning to believe and accept the good things God says about us.

To officially kick things off, we should probably start by going to the source that unites us – the Bible. What better place could there be to look for an understanding about our worth? The Bible describes our worth as something that's intrinsic, or "built-in" to who we are. Something that can't be separated from us, no matter what we do. It's there even when we're full of shame, guilt, and hypocrisy – when we've been rejected, disowned, or written off as insignificant.

The book of Genesis tells us that we were formed in the very image of God. The Psalms tell us that we are fearfully and wonderfully made. Ephesians tells us that God chose us before the foundations of the earth were even formed, and that we are His possession, chosen for the praise of His glory, and that we have an inheritance in Heaven with Him as His children. Perhaps the most well-known verse of all, John 3:16, tells us that we are so valuable in God's eyes that He sent His only son to die in our place. This alone should tell us something about our value, because value is often defined by what someone else is willing to pay. The lengths God was willing to go to in order to redeem us are a direct reflection of what we are worth to Him.

The question is, do we believe any of this? Sort of. We believe it kind of like we believe that Paris is the capital of France. It's knowledge that's stored in our heads, but it's not affecting us in a way that's real to us. What we are affected most by is the nagging voice of our inner skeptic, speaking in a voice that seems louder, more constant, and more convincing than any other. In our darkest moments, we just aren't able to believe what we desperately want to.

Some of it comes from the false idea we have of what it means to be objective. Somehow, it has been ingrained into us that the only real type of honesty is brutal honesty, and that, in order to be "truthful" with ourselves, we must be zooming in on some fault or failure of ours. This is why we can't take a compliment and why we tend to take criticisms to heart. It's also why, when we look in the mirror, it's so much easier to notice the things we don't like.

The crow's feet, the wrinkles, the extra pounds, and the baggy eyes. What don't we see? Our self-worth.

In a way, we don't even like the term "self-worth," because it contains a certain word that we Christians are very bothered by – the word "self." We've grown up believing that we shouldn't think too often, too highly, or too seriously of ourselves, and that a self-focus is, well… selfish. We've been told that we should deny ourselves. Of course, all of these principles are good and valid when taken in the proper context.

However, we often mistake them to mean that we should ignore our unresolved questions about our value. This, of course, is foolishness, because, to deny our own importance would be to deny the very thing Christ sacrificed Himself for. We are the reason He came to earth.

And yet, many of us have grown up believing that the only thing valuable about us is "Christ in us." This has often created the impression that we are merely worthless vessels – mass-produced clones, eagerly waiting for God to fill us so that we can finally be made valuable and distinct. Until then, well… sorry. You ain't worth too much, kid. Of course, this isn't inaccurate, because we know that God saw value in us BEFORE we were saved. As it is said, "While we were yet sinners, Christ died for us."

There are many reasons we may doubt our self-worth, and some of them actually have good indications. For example, some of us feel bad about ourselves, not because we are bad people, but because we are good people. So good that we could never live up to our good expectations! Our self-disapproval actually points to higher motives. After all, only a complete narcissist would look at all of his shortcomings and feel totally fine about them.

Of course, there are those of us who struggle with self-worth who don't even know it. If you asked us, we'd say we are fine, and that we have no doubts about our value. We might even pass a polygraph test saying it. And yet, though we deny the illness, the symptoms show. They are: perfectionism. Perpetual busyness. Overreactions to criticism. An incessant need to be right. People-pleasing. A dependence on others for approval. In these areas, our low self-approval shows itself, betraying our nicely-polished answers.

One problem is that we only become aware of our self-worth struggle once something forces it to surface. We are struck by a misfortune. We lose the job that made us feel important. Now, without the money... without the fancy title... without the aspirin to take care of the symptoms, we suddenly can no longer deny our illness. Now, if we were to take that same polygraph test, we would say: we are no longer sure.

I feel that the whole self-worth quest was summed up for me one day when I watched a movie called Peaceful Warrior. It is about a young man who discovers that throughout his life, he had based his sense of self-worth on his ability to outperform his peers and achieve excellent results. Only once he ends up shattering his leg and losing his ability to achieve, does he discover that he no longer feels valuable. He begins to discover that his value never was in his abilities or his image, and begins his own quest towards true self-acceptance.

It demands a completely different mindset from him, because it requires him to strive less, rather than more. It feels totally illogical and counterintuitive, which is why he struggles to make headway. Of course, the same is true for us. This quest is about learning how NOT to strive – learning to be at peace with ourselves just as we are. And, for those of us who are used to pushing hard for results, this journey may feel like utter foolishness. It is a frustrating, slow process, which is why we often abandon it short of reaching our goal.

To make headway, we may have to overcome some of our preconceived notions about what self-worth is. Too many self-help gurus have made this quest seem like a game – one that can be won by looking in the mirror and saying, "I'm good, I'm great, I'm wonderful." Don't worry, that's not what this book will ask you to do. In fact, it might even ask you to do something of the opposite – to look at your flaws objectively and to see them boldly, while realizing that they don't subtract one bit from your overall value.

So, at the risk of offending some, or sounding too self-indulgent to others, we will now take an objective look at the subject of self-worth, and do so from a Biblical perspective (if you're open to the idea that that's possible). If so, then you've come to the right place.

There is a lot of pertinent information here for you, or for anyone who desires to be more certain of his/her value. Without further ado, let's begin!

CHAPTER 1

SELF DOUBT – THE LOSS THAT KEEPS ON TAKING

There's no doubt that it is a problem when our value is questioned. The feeling alone can cause us a great deal of pain. And, as though this weren't enough, it's really only the beginning, because, from here, the problem unleashes a plethora of new problems that snowball into our lives.

1. LONELINESS

When a person doubts his worth, he is doubting that he has anything to offer, which greatly affects the way he relates to people. It usually causes him to have either too few relationships or to have relationships that lack intimacy and vulnerability. This, in turn, leaves him feeling lonely. Loneliness has less to do with the quantity of relationships we have than the quality, which is why we sometimes find it possible to still feel lonely even when we're surrounded by people. It's also why certain celebrities admit that they, despite being well-known and well-loved, still manage to feel very lonely through it all. Comic sensation, Robin Williams, despite his fame and success, actually felt like a prisoner in his own mind. Hit singer and legend, Michael Jackson, once confessed to putting mannequins in his room so that he wouldn't feel so alone. How strange that those who have all the trappings of success can still doubt their own value. Maybe we could learn something from this – that real worth is something that's already in us. If we know that, we are already wealthy beyond measure. If we don't, no amount of money, fame, or success can give it to us.

2. TIMIDITY

When people doubt their value, they may also become timid. They may lack the self-assurance required to be confident in social settings, decision making, and self assertion. A person is less likely to stand up for his convictions if he isn't sure that they matter. He won't feel permitted to voice his thoughts at work or at church or when talking politics with his friends. He may think the problem is theirs or that it has to do with the circumstances, but really, it is rooted in his own feelings of unworthiness.

3. RECKLESSNESS

Another problem of lost value is that it makes us less likely to think we are worth preserving. A man who doesn't value what he has will act like he has nothing to lose. He won't go to the gym if he doesn't value his body. He won't go to church if he doesn't value his soul. He will not do much of anything that requires intention, willpower, or stepping out of his comfort zone, and he'll probably indulge in all the more harmful things that feel good, like cholesterol, sugar, and alcohol. He won't be concerned about the consequences, because they don't threaten anything that he values.

4. DEFENSIVENESS

This is another common problem that comes from not knowing one's self-worth. If we aren't sure of our value, we'll be far more likely to believe it is where it is not, and, to become extremely defensive of those things we think it is in. If a woman finds worth in her beauty, she may take it to heart when others fail to validate her for it. In her mind, what people say of her beauty, she truly believes they're saying of her worth.

5. BLAMING

Blaming is what we do when our sunsets no longer stir us. It's also what we may do when we don't feel valuable, or when something in us seems to be lacking. Since we feel a lack, we feel the need to justify it by having something to point at. This lets the world know that we are excused for any obvious weaknesses, and that they are the fault of someone or something else.

6. DISTRACTION

Another problem of not feeling valuable is distraction. If we haven't found our self-worth, our constant search for it will always be interfering with more important searches like, our search for God, our search to hear His voice, or to know where He is leading. Trying to do all of this at once splits our focus in too many directions. It'd be like trying to play football while also trying to make an important phone call. You won't do either thing well.

16

Similarly, you and I will only exhaust ourselves physically, emotionally, and mentally if we never figure out where our value really lies.

7. MISPLACEMENT

Not knowing our true value has the potential to lead us astray. Maybe you're not meant to be an accountant, but you're too afraid of your family's reactions if you ever chose a different path. This is where they think you belong, and it's where you find their value and support. But, staying there means that you're not experiencing the growth and purpose of the path that God wants you on. Not having your own sense of value is what keeps you from moving, too dependent on a stream of validation that others control.

8. IMPAIRMENT

As the flight attendant will always say, in the event of an accident, you should secure your own oxygen mask before helping others secure theirs. This concept also applies to the subject of self-worth because if you've found your own self worth, you'll be able to help other people find theirs. You'll be able to convince them that it's real if you yourself are convinced. But if you haven't even been able to help yourself, you probably won't be able to help anyone else out here either.

DEFINITIONS

Hopefully, we see that the doubting of our worth is a threat to be taken seriously. One with many consequences. One that can attack any age group, demographic, class and culture. It can affect the poor and downtrodden just as it can affect the rich and successful.

But what exactly is self-worth? How could we define it? Many of us, when we hear the term, think of "self-esteem," but, self-esteem refers to the way we feel about ourselves. It's something that can change depending on how we feel. Self-worth on the other hand, refers to something that cannot change, no matter what we are feeling. Even when we have no self-esteem, we still have self-worth.

Self-compassion is another term that we hear a lot of these days. It deals with a certain double standard that exists in many of us. We see others as valid recipients of patience, kindness and forgiveness, but not ourselves. To learn to give those things to ourselves is to learn self-compassion.

Self-confidence refers to how much (or how little) we trust our own capabilities. A man can trust that he is capable of running in that marathon in November, yet still wonder if he has any value as a person. He can lack self-esteem while still being rich in self-confidence.

Self-efficacy is another term that we commonly hear. It is a lot like self-confidence, only it describes more than a simple belief in one's own capabilities. It also measures the level of strength in that belief.

Many of us confuse self-worth with pride. We're afraid that if we believe in our own value, it might make us narcissists. Or that, if we trust our capabilities too much, it might make us arrogant. The truth, however, is that arrogance and narcissism actually stem from a person not knowing his own worth enough, rather than being too well acquainted with it. When a person feels he is lacking, he'll go to great measures to compensate for that lack.

Now that we've defined a few important terms and given attention to some of the pitfalls of feeling worthless, let's take this quest in the direction of observing which outside influences affect us most. When it comes to what we believe about ourselves, there are few things that are as persuasive as:

CHAPTER 2

THE INFLUENCE OF OTHER PEOPLE

It's eight o'clock in the morning in Washington, DC. Most people are starting their day. The roads fill up with traffic. Pedestrians take to the streets. On some corners, beggars meet them with held out hands, asking for change.

One man sets up to play his violin in the subway station. As he begins drawing his bow across the strings, beautiful sounds reverberate off of the subway walls. Most people are too rushed to notice. A few stop to watch or to throw spare change into his violin case. But what they don't realize is that the man before them is no ordinary street musician. His name is Joshua Bell, and he is one of the most celebrated classical musicians of our time – one that people from all over the world pay good money to watch play.

This test, called the Subway Experiment, was designed to see whether average people would be able to recognize hidden greatness on their own. But of the hundreds who passed Mr. Bell, only six stopped to listen. Only twenty gave any money at all. At the end of his forty-five minute session, Bell had only earned what an average street musician might earn.

What can we conclude by all of this? For starters, that the average person doesn't make a good talent scout. We seem to need a bit of help when it comes to finding those proverbial diamonds in the rough. This turns out to be pretty bad news for most of us who don't have the added benefit of being able to call ourselves world class violinists. The odds are even slimmer for us that we'll be noticed and appreciated for all that we are. Yes, God's image is in us, and yes, we have divine traits. We're loaded with inner beauty, purpose, and uniqueness, but there's just one problem – that's not what anybody is likely to notice us for.

In this world, we simply won't always be seen or valued for who we are. It's a fact that we can pretty much count on. And, it is important to note that no matter how thick-skinned we think we are, we are affected by this. Not because we're shallow, unbalanced, weak, or flawed, but because we were created this way. We have certain needs that are unique to our species.

A turtle will never care if it isn't shown love. It doesn't need to be held by its mother or nurtured when it is born. It just hatches from an egg and goes out into the wild. Humans, however, are wired much differently. From the moment we are born, our very survival depends on being shown a certain amount of love and attention. If a baby isn't held, it can literally cease to grow. It may even die if this persists too long.

We need to know that we matter, long before we're even old enough to start wondering why. This isn't about being thick-skinned or having a strong enough mental disposition. It's about a fundamental need that's central to our growth as humans – the need to know we have value.

Some of us haven't been told that we matter. We've been told in roundabout ways that we are insignificant. Perhaps, by someone in our lives who indirectly conveyed to us that we weren't important enough for their time. Perhaps someone made us feel that we were incapable of doing anything right. Somebody may have abandoned us, or abused us – mentally, emotionally, verbally, or physically.

Each of these experiences has taught us something about our value and has had a large bearing in how we define ourselves overall. Because, while we'd love to believe what God says about our worth, we're too haunted by how worthless we've been in someone else's eyes.

Others have a huge impact on how we see our own value. They either make it easier for us to feel valuable by accepting us, remembering us, and encouraging us, or they make it harder for us to feel valuable by rejecting us, forgetting us, or discouraging us. While they may not affect our worth, they sure do affect how we see it.

Most of the assessments made of us are made silently. As with Joshua Bell, nobody actually comes up to us, saying "hey dude, I think you're pretty average." Rather, they express their approval (or lack thereof) by what they *don't* say or do. They may withhold their acceptance of us and give it freely to someone else, making it clear that we aren't quite as high up in their book.

Some of them are trying to control us, hoping that we'll bend and contort ourselves to fit into the dull, unimaginative boxes that their minds can understand.   Usually, these are people who don't understand their own worth, and consequently, can't understand ours.

But our value is in who we are, who God made us, the traits He instilled in us, and the great lengths He went through to save us. These factors are far more crucial than any that the world looks at. Unfortunately, they don't seem to factor into how we are assessed.

The sad truth is that if you want to be recognized in any positive way – by your peers, by employers, by society, or by most anyone else in this world – you cannot simply be yourself. You have to be something better. Something more impressive. Less exposed. Something no one might see right through with the possibility of rejecting. Something that sits up straighter and that never says the wrong thing. Something that wins medals and impresses crowds with beauty, talent, or a trim figure. What is it? Who cares, as long as it gains you appreciation. Until you become what people value, the world will continue to define you by what they see. And what do they see?

Your flaws, mistakes, and imperfections. That one time in a hundred when you weren't on your game. Your co-workers still remember you for that time you fell asleep at your desk. The guys at the gym still remember you as the player who missed the game-winning shot. Your wife still remembers that time you mistook a wrench for a pair of pliers, and your parents still remember you as that kid who needs to be told when to wear a jacket.

No earthly friend is *so* great that he will always remember to tell you how much you matter, or give you affirmations that aren't in some way conditional. The encouragement you receive here will always be contingent upon your level of performance, or upon other people's fluctuating ability to see objectively.

No wonder it's so hard for us to see ourselves through God's eyes. All our lives, we've been bombarded with flawed, limited, or untrue assessments. None of them fully convey the depth of beauty, value, and uniqueness in who we are. It's why we no longer believe our value is there and why we don't recognize this for the great tragedy it is.

CHAPTER 3

THE RESULT

A while back, my wife and I became interested in home renovation shows. One of them, called Rehab Addict, involved a woman named Nicole Curtis who would renovate homes by restoring them to their original charm.

At first sight, the homes she worked on looked like lost-causes. They had cracked-brick walls, cheap, warped paneling, and outdated features. But each time, she would somehow end up turning these misfits into masterpieces.

Yet I noticed that her best touch-ups usually didn't involve adding anything to the home. Rather, it involved taking something away – some cheap cover that hid an artistic railing, or a cheap wall that covered old original woodwork.

Such findings would astound her, because she didn't understand how anyone could have covered such beautiful originality with such tacky, artificial facades. When I look at our lives, I wonder if the same may be true for us.

In each of us is God's image. We have His character, and nature, and purpose. We have uniqueness and personal beauty, but it all flies under the radar. It's like we are priceless original paintings, stuck in a world that doesn't value art. So, to be valued, we've learned that we must cover our artwork over with flashy exteriors that people notice. Suddenly, we start getting the appreciation we long for.

Many of us don't know we're wearing a cover. We've been wearing one so long that we see it as part of ourselves. We truly do think that our cover represents us, which is why we take it so personally whenever we're criticized or feel more worthwhile when we're affirmed.

We may wear covers because we feel lonely or inadequate. We may not want people to go out of their way for us, so we hide from them the true states of our hearts and minds, pretending that things are much greater than they really are. And, as extensive as our reasons for wearing covers, are the types of covers we wear. Do you wear a cover?

Maybe yours is your title. You went to great lengths to become a cop, an athlete, a college graduate. You've worked for your title, and now your title works for you. It tells the world: "I'm smart. I'm athletic. I'm gifted and dedicated". But it also says; "I'm afraid you might not like me if I didn't give you a reason". Silently, you wait for moments in the conversation when you can slip something in about your accomplishments. Until others are aware of your shiny cover, you feel naked and vulnerable.

Perhaps you wear a cover to protect yourself from critical people. You know they'd despise you if they saw how different you are, so you pretend not to have many opinions. To avoid opposition, you blend in with your opponents. You keep everything impersonal with casual chatter, avoiding anything that hints of meaning. You've mastered the art of redirecting a conversation back to shallow waters, should it threaten to go too deep. The weather, the news, or celebrity gossip. You think you're saving face, but you're really just hiding.

Or perhaps your cover hides your strengths. Just as you've learned not to stand out in bad ways, you've learned that it's just as dangerous to stand out in good ways. That's why, even though you know the answer to that tough question your boss is asking, you won't raise your hand. Others might fear you or ostracize you for shining brighter than them.

Maybe you just like to look normal. You want the world to know you're as cool and confident as the name-brand clothes you wear. Behind your cool outer layers are more cool inner layers, stretching all the way to a cool inner core behind which are no surprises, bizarre parts, or eccentricities. What you see is what you get, right? Sure... if only.

Maybe your cover is one of perfection. You wear it to shield yourself from negative attention at church. Even though you'd rather be anywhere else, even though you're hurting, confused, and afraid, even though your teenager is battling with doubt and addiction, you pose with a smile fit for the cover of "Perfect Christian Magazine", and a posture that says; "I've got it all together". Deep down though, you just hope things will be okay and think that the key must lie in pretending they already are.

Maybe your cover is one of pretending not to care what people think of you. You tell the world that you're thick-skinned and unafraid of vulnerability. But is that true? If so, why is it so important for people to know this? Wouldn't it be easier not to care what they think?

Maybe you hide behind parts of yourself that you know others like. They think you're smart and funny, so you display your wit and humor as though they alone are what define you. You wear the traits others accept like a shield to hide the traits they'd never understand. You're terrified of letting them see there's more to you, like a serious side? A poetic side? A hurting side.

Maybe your cover is in someone else. It's your kids' accomplishments that you stand behind. What they do indirectly points to you. Their good grades reflect your brain. Their home runs reflect your strength. But their failures point to you as well, which is why you're so embarrassed when one of them is struggling and why you feel shame instead of the appropriate amount of sadness or concern.

Whatever your cover is, it makes it easier for you to feel valued and for others to see your value. It removes the guesswork for them. It lessens the risks of being passed over by a world that will probably never see your true colors or care much about them even if they did.

The biggest problem with the cover is that it becomes our top priority. In times of crisis, when our efforts should be focused on solving a significant problem, we instead focus on burying the problem. This is when a closet alcoholic conceals the habit that is slowly killing him or when a struggling couple avoids going to a counselor, both for fear of what their friends might think.

In these Christians' lives (and in many of our lives), the cover, whichever one it may be, has ascended to the level of idolatry. Even as our lives are nearing ruin, we're still worried about appearances. This would be like the captain of a sinking ship being concerned about a cosmetic blemish on his boat, not noticing the more dire issue at hand.

In the second book, *The Power Of Remembering*, we talked about how common it is for people to give in to despair without ever crying out for help. This is a common reason why. Because no one really knows them beyond their covers, no one is able to recognize the despair they're in.

Sometimes when we fall in front of our friends, we stand back up and laugh before we even know if we're hurt. We pretend it was intentional, because it hurts more to have a vulnerability exposed than to suffer a physical bruise. We're scared to be seen doing anything we didn't plan. To be caught singing when we didn't know someone was listening, or to make eye contact with someone for just a split second too long. We are so used to living beneath our covers, in the safety of controlling which parts people can see, which parts they can't.

Something is missing. Or maybe, it's not gone – just covered over. Pushed deep beneath a surface we thought we needed to wear in order to be valued. Funny, because beneath that surface is where our greatest value lies. Anything we cover ourselves with is of far less worth.

CHAPTER 4

A FLAWED SYSTEM

In short, our sense of self-worth depends a lot on how we measure up on society's system, which defines us by things like the size of our paychecks, the size of our homes, and how far we can throw a ball. It also factors in how well we're behaving, how hard we're working, and how much we're contributing. Basically, it is a system of comparing. If we score high enough in meeting all of these criteria, we are deemed valuable in society's eyes. If we score lower, we are seen as less valuable.

40

This system isn't only used by society. It is also used by us in our own self-assessments. We too find our worth by comparing ourselves to others. Usually, we sort everybody into two main groups that we compare ourselves to – one that is full of good, prosperous, successful people that we aspire to be like, and another that is full of bad, despicable, repulsive people who we think we are better than. We typically rank ourselves as being somewhere in the middle. And usually, our motivation is to move closer to that good group, and to keep from sliding any further into the bad group.

All in all, we like this system. It is the fairest one we know of. It judges people non-discriminately, labeling them by their actions. No need for sympathy or pity. If a person ranks low in this system, it is only because he has done something to earn it. Yet, despite how fair this system seems, it is actually very dangerous. It tends to make human value into a thing that is earned, rather than endowed, and it leaves no room for grace.

For a moment, let's take this discussion towards a man named Francis "Two-gun" Crowley. Crowley was a career criminal who once blazed a trail of robberies, home invasions, gunfights, and murders through New York. He was a heartless killer who wouldn't think twice to level anyone in his path. He is one that most of us would easily look down upon and who, by our system, would be rightfully labeled as a less-valuable person.

Now, let's ask ourselves something... is a man like this really less valuable? Before you answer or go straight to making that point about how some crimes are greater than others in God's eyes, let's remember that we're not talking about guilt here, or about the extent to which a person deserves punishment. We're talking about one thing: Value – Christ sees it in all of us, enough to where each of us were worth dying for – you, me, the prostitute at the well, and the thief who was crucified next to him. Surely, a man like Crowley is no exception.

The truth is that if we struggle to see the worth in some people or if our own sense of value comes by comparing, it proves that we don't really understand our value at all. It may do us well to look at the New Testament and to remember that Christ equated us all to murderers if we have hated our brother. He equated us all to adulterers if we have lusted in our hearts. He rebuked the pious religious leaders who thought they were better than everyone else because of their good deeds and records, and He gave forgiveness to anyone who repented, regardless of their pasts.

Christ told us to pray for our enemies. He told us to visit those in prison. He didn't tell us to pump up our own egos by comparing ourselves to them, which is what we so often do. We use our flawed system to distinguish ourselves from the world's wretches, but Christ seems to want to lump us all into the same pot together. He wants to eradicate this thinking that some of us can be more valuable, or that our actions can make us any less in need of Grace.

We should reconsider our most common ways of determining value. Our actions leave us all falling short of grace, and not a single inch closer to being redeemable, no matter how great and wonderful we think we are. So maybe we should stop determining worth by actions, and instead, let it be based on who we are.

CHAPTER 5

WHO WE ARE

We were made in God's image. Our hearts thrive on love, joy, and peace. We yearn to be in harmony with nature, with each other, and with God. No human enjoys pain. No one loves heartache. We each have eternity etched into our hearts. And, each man has a conscience within him. A silent voice, leading him in the direction of happiness. This, we might say, is a description of our design.

And yet, it seems that so few of us match this description. It's far easier to find people who aren't living for the eternal, but for the moment. People who are acting immorally, violently, and selfishly.

You'd almost guess that our design was to hurt each other and steal each other's possessions. Sometimes it's easy to wonder – is this really the race God made in His own image? And if so, how do we explain this? Maybe, it has to do with the fact that we are not in the world we were made for.

When you take any creature out of its intended environment, it becomes hard for that creature to act as it was meant to. Take a fish out of the sea. Will it swim gracefully? Will it glide effortlessly, the way it would underwater? No. It will succumb to gravity, flop around, and collect debris.

The world without sin, pain or death, was the one where we swam gracefully, and it wasn't such a struggle for us to live out our design. There was no fear, pain, or death. God walked in physical form. We could walk with Him. Talk with Him. Now though, in this fallen world, we are eternal beings in a temporary place.

Bearers of a holy God's image in a foreign, hostile environment. In short, we are fish out of water.

And yet, we need to remember that a fish out of water is still a fish, even though it's not acting like one. You wouldn't call it a frog, just because on land, it may look more like one. It would still have a fish's DNA. It would still have all the instincts, traits, and needs of a fish.

And we, despite our strange actions, are still God's design. Still made in His image. We're still the ones that He sent His only Son to save. Don't you see? While our actions can change, our design cannot. And, since our worth is etched into the fabric God designed us with, our worth cannot change either.

This explains a few important things. First, why the world has missed our value – they haven't been looking. But also, we haven't been showing them. We've been showing them this crazy, unnatural type of behavior, stemming from being here in this world with fears, pain, and heartaches we were never meant to know. Crowley is the extreme example of this, but we must remember that even he was made in God's image. Even he had eternity written into his heart.

In the highly-acclaimed self-help book, *How To Win Friends And Influence People*, Crowley is briefly mentioned. The author talks about this criminal's capture, and a note that he left behind for whoever it may concern. The note said, "Under my coat is a weary heart, but a kind one. One that would do nobody any harm." These don't sound like the words of a killer, and the author uses this as proof to illustrate that Crowley was a narcissist, as well as a thug. But, I have wondered many times if there was a different explanation.

Maybe it's proof of something more – that even this brutal thug could see that there was a better version of himself than the one he had shown the world. Maybe some deep part of him was trying to say, "I'm sorry. You haven't seen the real me. I haven't *been* the real me."

Most of us, if we're honest, can relate. No, not in the way that we've gone on public shooting sprees, but in the way that we know we haven't always been who we were made to be. We haven't always acted as we've known we should or as we were designed to. We also know that the world has based our worth upon its snapshots of us during our worst moments – those times when we've lost our cool and said hurtful things that we didn't mean, when we've bent the truth or failed to keep our promises, when we've quit too soon, or despaired in our struggles. By our own standards, we all could be called liars, frauds, and hypocrites. We all could be made to feel that our value is in some way less because of it. But, thank goodness... our value isn't changed by our actions.

On January 21, 1932, Crowley's life came to an end. He was brought to the electric chair to be executed. Some people rejoiced as he was strapped into the chair, and shortly thereafter, as his soul left the earth.

No one seemed to think that there was any loss in such a man's passing. But this is where we are wrong. There is a loss anytime any human is kept from living the life he was meant to. Only sometimes do we see it.

When a person dies of cancer, we don't rejoice that the cancer is gone. We acknowledge the loss of a valuable person, and we mourn it. In the same way, we lose a valuable person when evil keeps someone from being who he was made to be.

You see, it's not that some of us have value and others don't. It's that some of us live our entire lives without realizing it, or discovering the fullness of knowing it. The bottom line is, whether we see it or not, there is something very valuable in every single one of us.

CHAPTER 6

THE REMEDY

The problem isn't just that we lose sight of our worth, but also, all the silly things we do to try to get it back. Many of us, in an attempt to feel worthwhile, put all of our effort into climbing higher on life's ladder. We'll try to make ourselves smarter, more-accomplished, better-paid, more-involved at church, or more self-sufficient.

Many of us have climbed pretty high on this ladder, and we've acquired some impressive qualities, should anyone dare to question our worth. But now, at this impressive pinnacle we've ascended to, Christ speaks to us with some rather backwards-seeming news. He says, "You must become like children." Wait a minute... did we hear Him right?

Doesn't He mean we're supposed to go out and sign ourselves up for more church events, get a whole lot busier, stress ourselves out with even more worthwhile endeavors, and then, toss a few extra bucks into the offering bucket? That's what normally puts us back into good standing – with ourselves and with our peers. Is Christ really saying that this is unnecessary? And even stranger, why on earth is He telling us to be more like children?

Children get caught stealing cookies. They hit each other and misbehave. They sometimes lie when they're in trouble and steal each other's toys. Why is He telling us that they're the ones we should emulate? It seems absurd, but then again; Christ also said

He would use the simple to confound the wise. We think we're wise. They're simple. This sure is confounding.

As usual, Christ was speaking somewhat figuratively. When He spoke of children, He wasn't referring to age, but I believe, to the blank slates we started out as. The pure, unadulterated versions of ourselves that existed before our hearts became muddied up and scribbled over, and have stopped looking like they should.

Many of us know this. We can tell that despite all of our accolades and our great strides forward, there is still something precious that we've only gotten further from, rather than closer to. We know it in our hearts, and we've spent significant portions of our lives trying to get back what we once had, not really sure what that is.

Christ tells us where to look, but His instructions go against our logic. What He tells us to do is similar to what they do on those home renovations shows, where value is found by subtracting, not adding. We too can discover what's in us by stripping away things like our covers. Our facades. Our false ways of trying to gain value, justification and importance.

Children represent the beautiful, handcrafted woodwork that lies beneath our tacky makeovers. They display a clear picture of that nature we've forgotten. They have a special ability to trust. They don't stress and worry over every step, and can enjoy life as it happens. They have a keener sense of what's right and wrong, and aren't as quick to rationalize bad behavior.

Children aren't yet corrupted or perverted by the things we get tangled up in. They don't yet have the unnatural addictions to sin, pornography, or destructive substances, which we can only acquire with age.

Children have an amazing ability to hope. They're better and quicker at forgiving. They see the wonder in small things that you and I overlook. And, they usually speak their minds more honestly and without any filter.

The "childlike state" Christ is referring to is not a place of perfection, but a place of imperfect innocence. A place of single-mindedness and wholeheartedness. And no matter where we're headed, this should be included in our destination.

I believe Christ used children as our example for a number of reasons, but largely, because it's where we all came from. No matter who you are or where you're from...if you're Two-Gun Crowley or Mother Teresa, you were still once a child playing with toys, reliant upon your parents for support and protection. And before that, you were an infant, staring helplessly up into your mother's eyes.

No man's history is void of youth. No villain ever skipped childhood to become a villain. No outlaw skipped infancy to become an outlaw. And you want to know what? That value and nature that children display… it's still in us. In essence, Christ is saying; "Have you lost touch with that? You'll find it if you look back at where you came from." In your heart, become like a child.

Christ exemplified children because He understood that you and I are always looking for a comparison. It seems to be in our nature to base our self-assessments on where we stand next to our fellow man. In a way, He's saying; "Do you want to know where you really stand? Stop looking at your neighbor. Stop looking at that jailbird. Start looking at children".

His message was good news, because it told us that our value is intrinsic. It isn't in how much or how little we make. It has nothing to do with what our families think of us – our spouses, kids, or our parents. It has nothing to do with which side of the prison walls we find ourselves on. It's always in us, and there is always a way back to it, no matter how far we've fallen.

Become like a child. This is the ultimate statement of our intrinsic value. It means that real progress won't be a continuation in that same direction. Going forward will actually be a backward motion of some kind. Not a *doing* of anything, but a major *undoing* of what's been done.

There is one more aspect to this, and I believe it's the biggest yet. I believe the main reason Christ exemplified children was because they represent the start of life, which is the one place where value is easily seen. We love things when they are new!

When you see a puppy, a fawn, or a colt, you see something that's easy to admire, something you don't have to force or contrive, and which doesn't require reason. You don't need reasons to love an infant. You don't love it for how well it can play the violin. You simply love it for what it is.

We tell children to be themselves. We tell them there is nothing better they could ever hope to be. We tell them there's no act they could put on that would ever make them greater. No facade they could wear that could make them shine brighter than who they genuinely are.

Then, at some point, all these things we tell them stop being true. They leave childhood and they cross an imaginary line, entering a world where their worth is suddenly contingent upon their performance and their behavior. Suddenly, their creativity, their character, their passions, their hearts, and their uniquenesses are all overshadowed by just one thing - their ability to prove themselves in the real world. Their human value stops being seen as intrinsic.

If you look at the problems that arise in life, you'll see that most of them begin to happen here – when a person stops believing in his own value. Because, when our value is seen, we believe in it and act on it. When it's not seen, we either begin to increase our performance, or we begin to doubt that our value is within reach, and we begin to wander from it.

Why is this? At what point did we decide that it's okay to treat human value like it's a privilege reserved for youth? This, I believe, is a huge mistake we've made in our perspectives, and it's one that Christ is addressing when He tells us to observe (and be like) children.

CHAPTER 7

A PERSONAL ACCOUNT

At this point, I'd like to go back to that question that I talked about at the beginning of this book. You know, the one that my counselor asked me... "Caleb, do you know what you like about yourself?" I would finally begin exploring that question just a few short weeks after he asked it.

I was on vacation in the Boundary Waters in northeast Minnesota with a group of friends from my church. Our plans were to spend a week in the wilderness, camping and fishing by day, and sleeping under the stars at night. For me, it felt like a much-needed break from the monotony of life. And it was a chance to do a bit of soul-searching. By the glow of a fire. Beneath the Milky-Way's light. Would the answer to this question come to me? I had high hopes that it would.

During our first night, we stayed at the Outfitters lodge in downtown Ely, Minnesota. After a good night's sleep, we woke at sunrise and headed to the water's edge, making our final preparations before setting out.

The weather was perfect. The day was going just as we had planned. Our canoes were half in the water, and our gear was loaded up in them. Everything seemed to be in order. We were about to push off, when Dave, our group leader, gave me a strange look that I didn't quite understand. He then said, "Caleb, did you forget to bring your rubber boots?" I looked down at my feet, nestled in a pair of dingy sneakers I brought that I didn't care about getting dirty.

As his words registered, my heart sank to my toes. I now remembered the discussions we had had in our preparation meetings, and our specific instructions to bring rubber boots, but somehow, despite all of our planning, and all of our preparation, I had forgotten to bring mine.

I peered about at the group, not sure what to say. Everyone else had on their rubber boots. I was the only one who wasn't wearing any. I suddenly wished I had some fantastic explanation that would let me off the hook, and that would make everyone smile and pardon this classic misunderstanding. But, the only honest answer I could come up with was one that revealed how oblivious I was, and how starkly my memory paled in comparison to everyone else's. So, in an attempt to diffuse the situation, I said in a somewhat jovial way "Come on guys… it's just the wilderness." I looked around for a smiling face, but nobody was laughing.

Dave pulled me aside and spoke to me. He told me that I could borrow his boots if I needed to, as he had brought an extra pair. He also told me that if I had any questions in the future, I should feel free to ask. His approach was gentle. Well-intended. And yet, it somehow made me feel small, almost like I was a grade-schooler who had forgotten his homework, and now, was wearing a dunce-hat in front of the class.

Somehow, in this beautiful place where I'd hoped to find answers to my heart's burning questions, I instead only felt less certain than before. My sense of self-doubt was growing, not shrinking. What did I like about myself? I was even less sure now.

As we headed deeper into the wild, I tried to readjust my focus and to be more aware of the natural beauty around me. There were so many awesome sights to behold. And yet, in a way, it all gave me a strange sense of pressure. After all, if I can't feel good about myself out here, where can I? No matter how I tried to push them away, those ugly feelings of self-doubt seemed to be in my periphery, no matter where I looked.

As the week progressed, small things kept happening that reinforced those feelings. For example, I kept discovering new things that I had somehow forgotten to pack, like sunscreen, bug spray, and oh yeah... deodorant. I felt embarrassed and ashamed each time I had to ask to borrow something. I felt like this somehow defined me, and as though I had a sign taped to my forehead, spelling out the word "flawed".

Maybe it was the fact that I had gotten off on the wrong foot. Maybe it was the fact that everyone else seemed so good at remembering things, and I was the only one who was forgetting. Or, maybe it was those fears that had sprouted up in me while talking to my counselor, and the doubts of my likeability that had been growing like cancer ever since. For whatever reasons, I found myself fighting the battle of a lifetime to simply feel worthwhile.

Later on that week, I dropped my paddle into the water and nearly lost it for good. I had to swim after it in my clothes before it reached the rapids. Later that night, Dave saw me struggling in the dark, and lent me his head-lamp – another item I had forgotten.

But perhaps the worst moment of all came about three days into our trip, while we were paddling out to a secret fishing hole that Dave wanted to show us. We had been going for an hour and were about a third of the way there, when suddenly, I realized that I had forgotten my life vest back at camp.

This was something that Dave specifically said we should never do. He made it very clear to us that we shouldn't ever leave shore without our life vests on – no exceptions. Somehow, I had done just that.

I quickly peered about the canoe, hoping that I was wrong. Wishing I'd see it lying somewhere on the floor or beneath the fishing gear. But, deep down, I knew better. I knew it was right where I left it – leaning against the tree back at our campsite. How could I be so stupid? Now, I would once again have to face everyone and be outed as an idiot.

"Excuse me", I said aloud, getting everyone's attention. "Apparently, I forgot my life vest back at camp". Everyone looked at me. A few of them were smiling, as though they thought I was kidding and were waiting for a punch-line. Dave's smile slowly faded as he realized I was serious.

We halted and brought our canoes to shore, huddling to form a plan. The decision was made that two people would paddle back to retrieve the vest. I would stay and wait, being that it wasn't safe for me to travel back without one.

I sat there with Dave, waiting in the silence simply for time to pass. At this point, I wanted the earth to swallow me up. I felt so embarrassed. I hated myself for being so stupid. For causing so many problems. I believed everybody else felt the same about me.

My mind began to run amuck with self-accusations, and I started thinking things like, "Come on, Caleb… wake up. This is the real "you." The one that frustrates people. The one that tests everyone's patience, and eventually, drives them away." All of my mind's common judgments fell upon my heart like a ton of bricks, crushing any good thoughts that I was still struggling to hold onto.

But, I was suddenly snapped out of my trance by a faint, audible voice. Dave, just a few feet away, began to say something. He said the words, "Hey man, don't be down on yourself. It's not the end of the world."

I gave him a half-smile and quickly looked in the other direction. "Thanks Dave," I replied, not knowing what else to say. He was trying to be nice. I expected that much. Most people will offer such trite comforts simply so that they don't feel awkward in situations like these.

But Dave seemed determined to let me know that he meant it, and he seemed to sense that he wasn't getting through to me. It almost felt like he could see that I was hurting and that I needed to be reminded of my worth.

He came up closer and said, "I want you to know that everybody here loves you. Do you know that?"

"Yeah," I said again. "I know that." I gave another half-smile and looked away again. "Thanks, Dave," I said again, picking up a small stone and throwing it into the water, hoping he would just back off. But through the corner of my eye, I could see that he was still staring at me.

I was starting to feel even more uncomfortable. Why was he being so persistent about this? I got it. He forgave me. Now, the next step was moving on, so that this whole thing would start moving further behind us.

Suddenly, Dave got up to his feet. He started walking toward me. He stood right where I was looking, so that we were face-to-face. I felt so thankful for my sunglasses. They were the only thing I had to hide my shame-filled eyes.

Then, Dave reached his arms forward and put his hands on my shoulders. He said, "Everybody here loves you. Do you know that?" This time, I didn't respond. Perhaps, my cover had been blown. Perhaps I knew too well not to fib to someone who was standing so close to me.

Dave told me to take off my sunglasses. I did. He said "Look me in the eye." Slowly, I forced my eyes upward until at last, they met his. Then, in the most confident tone, he said, "I want you to know that I love you. Do you know that? I. Love. You."

Something inside of me froze. My guard-walls fell. For the first time in years, I sensed something greater than doubt penetrating through the walls of my heart. I sensed acceptance of who I was in a way that I actually believed.

And I knew that Dave wasn't just speaking to me. He was speaking to that hurting ten-year-old boy who sometimes felt like he was only a problem. He was speaking to the confused teenager, the young man, and the misunderstood adult all at once. Suddenly, tears started streaming down my face.

Dave pulled me in and held me in his arms. As I stood there for a good while in his embrace, I continued to cry a torrent of tears that had been building up in me. The wall had broken that held them. I believed what Dave was saying.

I believed that I had value, and that it didn't have to do with my performance or my deservedness or any other thing. All that I *knew* about my worth (which didn't seem real) suddenly became real. Dave looked me in the eye once more, as though he understood how badly I needed to hear it, saying, "Listen. I meant that. There's nothing you could do to change that."

And, right there, I thought of that question that my counselor had asked me, "Caleb, can you tell me what you like about yourself?" I felt like I finally knew the answer. The reason I liked myself was because… well, just because. Somehow, when you know that you are worthwhile, and you actually believe it, a funny thing happens – you stop needing reasons.

And maybe, this is the huge missing link in our quest to know our own value. We need more than a simple knowledge of our value. We need faith. Faith is what it takes for us to make that knowledge real.   Faith that our sins have truly been forgiven through Christ's blood. Faith that we are accepted in the beloved! Faith that because of Jesus, we are actually able to come boldly to the throne of grace.

CHAPTER 8

IMPORTANT LESSONS LEARNED

As someone who's struggled to know my own worth, I've often become very defensive whenever people have pointed out my faults. A lot of times, I've tried to deny those faults, even though, quite clearly, they exist.

Out there in those Northern woods, I saw them. I couldn't hide from them or deny them. I did, however, realize an important thing about them – that I often try to downplay them by highlighting other features that I'm proud of, like my humor, my intellect, or some ability that I possess. I try to keep up this balancing act where I   put my best put my best foot forward, hoping that others forget I have another foot.

But I've been learning that the good in our lives doesn't cancel out the bad. If I can create enough good qualities in me, it doesn't mean that my bad qualities suddenly stop existing. No amount of income, awards, or impressive features will make them disappear.

If my faults exist, then it means I have some things to work on, and work doesn't go away when you deny that it's there. When I'm in denial of my faults, I'm not fixing any problems. In fact, I'm fixing everything but the problem, and I'm missing valuable opportunities to work on those parts of me that need the most attention. While our faults don't change our worth, they sure do impair our ability to function.   I believe we cannot benefit from criticism until we understand this.

Dave helped me get this, and I'm beginning to see the large, integral role that people like him play in helping us see our value. Whether or not we believe we have worth, it is almost always because someone else led us to believe so. While our worth is God-given, our self-perspectives are inherited.

THE SEARCH FOR ENCOURAGING PEOPLE

It is important to have good, encouraging people in our lives. However, I've found that it's far easier to find unhelpful people, rather than people who are confident in who they are and who know how to handle vulnerability.

Sadly, this is true even within the church, where we shouldn't have to fear things like rejection or judgment. Church is a place where we teach about empathy, honesty, and transparency, so it is a natural assumption that here, we can safely take off our armor. And yet, despite what we teach, church is where some of our greatest cover-wearing takes place.

This may be due to some of the various pressures that Christians face – from the world and from each other. Since a large part of our calling is to be shining examples, we often feel that we must hide our our struggles, faults, fears, and hurts. Sometimes we deny these things even with ourselves, believing that such things are given power by our acknowledgments of them. Whatever the case, these factors are behind why church can be a place where vulnerability isn't always welcome or encouraged.

Many churchgoers, despite their great appearances and great intentions, simply have never learned to be vulnerable themselves. A lot of them have even been taught in their upbringings that vulnerability is a weakness. This is why even certain Christians will shun or judge you if you are transparent about a struggle. In their own lives, they were simply never given the freedom to be so open.

Some people want to be encouraging, but don't know how. Maybe they can't relate to your area of weakness. Others will invite your vulnerability, but not because they are interested in seeing you grow or develop. They more or less just enjoy having someone to relate to, because it makes them feel normal.

There are those who treat vulnerability like it's a one-way street. They invite you to be vulnerable, but would never dare be vulnerable themselves. They really are just silently comparing themselves to you to build up their own covers. If they can relate to any of your struggles, they will not tell you. They may even see your confessions as proof of their own moral superiority.

Of course, a lot of these people have no idea that they are doing this. In fact, they are often the people who give great first-impressions, and who, from an outside perspective, seem like the most loving parents, the most Godly leaders, and the most exemplary role models. And yet, on the inside, many of them are secretly struggling, hurting, and afraid.

This is why I am so thankful for Dave. Being a church leader himself, he could have easily chosen not to risk his image and reputation. But he did. When he saw my deep concerns, he prioritized them above his own. He wasn't afraid to risk hearing what I had to say. Nor did he see my vulnerability as a chance to stand on my shoulders and make himself feel more secure.

He helped me come out from under my cover, but in a way, he did so by coming out from under his. This showed a ton of bravery and strength, and I can't help but think of how much sturdier we'd all be if we had that kind of encouragement regularly. Do you have that in your life? I hope so. We all need that.

I've realized one more important thing in all of this – that since the world is so full of unsafe people, our covers actually serve a valuable purpose. In a metaphorical sense, we shouldn't take off our armor until we know we are out of the battle zone.

It isn't always wise or brave to be an open book. In fact, in most settings in life, our freest-flowing feelings and thoughts will not be welcomed, appreciated, or appropriate. Christ said we shouldn't cast our pearls before swine. Proverbs 4:23 says, "Guard your heart above all else, for it affects everything you do."

This quest isn't about learning to put our hearts out there for anybody, but about finding people who are trustworthy enough to have access to them – knowing who will nurture them, rather than stomp on them and add to their pain and sorrow.

Discernment is key. Wounds don't always come from enemies. Sometimes, what we feel hurt or betrayed by is actually the "wound of a friend," as the Proverbs say. These are better than the kisses of an enemy. When we feel betrayed, we must consider the source, and realize that a true friend is someone who has our best interests at heart, even when we ourselves do not.

CHAPTER 9

THE DESTINATION – SELF-ACCEPTANCE

I should mention that on one of our last days in the Boundary Waters, I had another great experience. It was completely different from many of the others that I mentioned. This time, I wasn't a burden or a nuisance. I was a hero. At least, for a few hours.

At the start of another sun-filled day, we loaded up our canoes and started paddling south. The bugs were starting to buzz around us a little more than they had been during the week, but they still weren't bad. In fact, we realized that we had actually come during the perfect window of time – somewhere between the first problematic onsets of neck-biting black-flies, and the last trailing snowflakes of winter that sometimes surprise campers early in the spring.

Like a gift from Heaven, it felt like we had been handed this lot of time, as well as this lustrous landscape to enjoy it in, with all of its sounds, smells, and reflections of God's beauty. Some, in the water. Others, in the sky.

After about an hour of steady paddling, we finally reached the base of a small falls that poured down a ledge where the incoming river narrowed. A bald eagle was staring at us from the top of a gnarly pine, just across the small bay which we parked our canoes and sat ashore of. We watched as we rested a few moments, snacking on some raisins and peanuts which we had packed into small Ziploc baggies. Then we tied our canoes securely, and each person went his own way. With my hat, my pole, and a few choice lures I had brought with me, I decided to hike a little further upstream than the others.

I forged my own trail upwards, hopping over large stones and breaking dead branches that barred the path. Occasionally, I would stop to cast. The turbulent waters I walked along were loud when you stood right by them. They demanded a sense of respect when you saw how quickly they pulled a lure. Sometimes, it felt like you had a fish, when really, it was just the current, mimicking the sensation of a fight.

After a couple of hours, we reconvened near our boats to see how everyone had fared in our individual attempts to catch dinner. To our surprise, no one had managed to catch a single thing. It was a little surprising that this spot had no fish to offer. I personally was not ready to accept this as a fact – that here, up in this immaculate wilderness between US and Canada, there wasn't a single hungry fish. That did not sit well with me.

I quickly decided that I needed to try even further upstream. I swapped lures and headed back up the trail I had tried earlier, only this time, I kept going. When I reached the top of the fast-moving water, the river opened up, and took a slower, more-peaceful tone. I could see right to the bottom in some of the deeper areas, and it felt like I had found a place promising.

I walked out to a rock that was situated in the middle of the river. To do so, I had to get my shoes and shorts wet. It would probably make for an unpleasant afternoon (especially if the temperature fell), but I felt that it would be worth it… especially if I were to catch a fish!

When I reached the rock, I stood atop it and made a few casts into the stiller, deeper waters. Suddenly, about twenty feet out, a shimmer of light reflected off a long, slender fish, which I realized was at the end of my line. There it was – the sign of life I was glad I had kept hope in.

My pole bent with fury as the fish raced outward, stretching my line. Slowly, after a few good minutes of fighting, it tired, and I brought it in. Not having a stringer, and being too far away from anyone else to ask for one, I pulled the lace off of one of my shoes and strung the fish up, tying it off on a small branch on shore. I went back to the rock I stood on to try for more.

It wasn't long before I had another. This time, a four-pound smallmouth that fought like it knew its dreadful fate on our dinner plates. After tiring him out, I strung him up by the shore along with the other. Again, I headed back out to search for more.

I caught another, and another. Soon, I had filled up the stringer with five fish! None of them were tiny. Each one could have given me bragging rights in some way.

With wet shoes, wet shorts, the pole I came with, and the small tackle box I had been toting, I tried now to hobble back down the path I had forged to get there, only this time, with the added burden of a shoestring full of five fish.

When I found the others, they were huddled together by the canoes. Only one of them was still fishing. Nobody had caught a single thing. Not one! So, when they saw me rounding the bend with five large fish, it was fair to say that I stood on the center of a pretty large stage.

Everybody raced over. They were asking me questions about where I had been and which lure I had used. I told them. With interests suddenly rekindled, each person in the group grabbed his pole and headed up to the glory hole I had told them about. I went back with them.

And, for about an hour, everybody sat right where I had sat, and fished right where I had fished, and nobody managed to catch a single thing. Nobody, except me. I ended up catching two more giants, both larger than any I had caught before. Now, I had pulled in a total of seven. The score was: Caleb: seven. Everyone else: Zilch. Not that anyone was counting.

We headed back that afternoon with only the fish I had caught. Some people were insisting that I had gotten lucky. Others were claiming that I must have had the right type of lure, which somehow, the fish all magically seemed to gravitate to. Dave leaned over and said, "Do you want to know what I think? I think you are simply a better fisherman than the rest of us." Then, he smiled and patted me on the back, saying, "Well done. You deserved this."

That night, as we had our smorgasbord of fried fish around the campfire, I felt like more of a man. I felt more valuable than I had before. I had proven myself. I didn't just win by a nose. I won by a landslide. And, I had become the guy that others depended on. It felt pretty good.

But, as I sat there, listening to the fire's faint crackles, I had a moment of pondering. I wondered why my sense of worth seemed to ebb and flow so dramatically, rising to such significant heights only when I shined more brightly than those around me. I realized as I sat next to those people I had camped with all week, that none of them really thought of me differently, despite my successes fishing. I was the only one who thought differently of myself. I felt like I had earned a right to be a part of the group, which I hadn't felt part of before.

I suddenly realized that in all my feelings of failure from earlier in the week, and in all of the attempts I had made to be funny or clever, compensating for what I felt I was lacking, there was really only one person I was trying to impress. Only one person I felt rejected by, and only one person who I so desperately craved the acceptance of: Myself.

Now, around the glow of this campfire, I was realizing that in order to have real happiness (and not the fake kind), I had to love myself and that I didn't even know how. I wondered... how could such an easy-sounding thing be so difficult? It was anything but easy. In fact, it felt like the challenge of a lifetime.

Perhaps I've learned to accept those feelings of worthlessness, or even rely on them. They've been a strong motivating force… to get ahead. To climb life's ladder. To be recognized as extraordinary. Funny how I've worked so hard, and in such roundabout ways, to gain my own approval.

In hindsight, I realize that I was right about something. If I couldn't feel good about myself there, even in one of the most beautiful, awe-inspiring places, there was no place on earth where I could feel good about myself.

But, I've realized that something of the opposite is also true – that if I can learn to feel good about myself anywhere, it doesn't matter where I go. I don't have to have captivating, wondrous surroundings. I just have to have an acceptance of myself. No matter where I go, I bring my self-acceptance or my self-condemnation with me.

As I write this, about a year since my trip to the Boundary Waters, I find that these lessons still hold true. I'm continually amazed by how difficult this quest really is, and how deep it goes. Despite the significant milestones that I've passed on the highway of self-acceptance, I find that I can quickly revert back to old unhealthy patterns of cover-wearing, comparing, ladder-climbing, and self-loathing.

It can be discouraging. It can cause me to wonder if I've learned anything at all from the amazing experiences I've had. And yet, despite the discouraging feelings that sometimes come, I am encouraged by something, and see that my efforts have not been for naught. I've learned a few ways to make this quest into a more reasonable, daily goal, which keeps me more consistent overall. Now, I will share with you some of the practical steps I have learned to take each day.

CHAPTER 10

IMPORTANT STEPS

1. GIVE

Giving is one of those things that reinforces our sense of self-worth. I find that when I give something, whether it be a dollar to a homeless man, or a smile to a stranger, I am reminded that I have something to offer. Also, I am blessed knowing that I have blessed somebody else.

If I make it a goal to make as little as two conscious, intentional giving gestures per day, even that small amount is enough to keep sense of self-worth balanced. Giving can include anything from volunteering in your community, to holding the door for an elderly person, to bringing your neighbor's newspaper to his front step.

2. THANK

That is, thank anyone you can think of for any kind thing that they have done for you, or any way in which they have blessed you. Thank your friend for being there for you. Thank your spouse for the little things she does. Thank that person at the supermarket who catches the door for you. Try to think of just two new things each day that you can thank somebody for.

Thanking could also be considered an act of giving, because, when we thank someone, we are giving them our appreciation. It is important that we are thankful for even life's smaller blessings, because as humans, we have an astounding capacity to take good things for granted.

Since a lot of our self-worth problems stem from noticing only life's negative aspects, we can begin to reverse this cycle by training ourselves to focus on the positive (which is what gratefulness gets us to do).

3. ACKNOWLEDGE

Look at your accomplishments. What have you achieved? For a lot of different reasons, many of us fail to do this simple task. Sometimes, it's because we are fear we may grow stagnant if we camp on our accomplishments too long. Other times, we don't think our accomplishments are worth noticing. Whatever the case, we rob ourselves of positive realizations which could sustain and grow our feelings of worthiness.

Acknowledge what you are good at – what you are gifted in, what you are purposed for, and what you've been given. By simply acknowledging these things, you are channeling your mind's energy in a way that fills your leaky self-worth tank, and hopefully, replaces some of the time spent fretting or speaking negatively, staring at your Android screen in a coma-like state.

4. SPEAK

In this case, don't just acknowledge what you've done – speak it over yourself. You can do this verbally or silently. Most likely, you'll find it easier to do it in your head. Simply remind yourself of your strengths and good traits, even when they don't seem true. Especially when they don't seem true. This is when you need it most.

Of course, please don't confuse this to mean that you should be fake with yourself or quote those ego-inflating one-liners that lack depth and personal relevance. You should be real with yourself. Hopefully you know by now, there is enough good stuff in you to be real about.

As you repeat these positive truths to yourself (which may not seem believable at first), they will become less foreign in time, and thus, become easier to believe. Make it a daily habit to proclaim the good truths you know.

5. ABSORB

While it is ultimately our own approval that we are seeking, this doesn't mean that we should cut ourselves off from the encouragement and positive reminders of others. It will always be of incalculable worth to have people in our lives who help us remember what is true.

Some people are great at this. They have eyes that are more practiced at seeing the good. They like to boost the morale of the people around them. If you know such people, keep them nearby. Make efforts to hold them inside your sphere of influence. Absorb all of their love and encouragement. In a way, you give to them by letting them give to you.

6. JOURNAL

Since my trip to the Boundary Waters, I've begun to keep a journal of my own positive traits. It includes accomplishments I've made that were challenging, tough races I've stayed in that would have been easier to drop out of. It includes memories of times when I was brave or strong, or when my character shined through in a good way. I easily forget these things if they're not written down.

I try to make it a habit to add to this list regularly, as well as to re-read it regularly. I'll read it when those feelings of unworthiness strike hard at random times, and for no rhyme or reason, I simply can't believe I'm valuable. I can't tell you how this journal has benefitted me, and how it helps me actually believe there's good in me, and that I'm not just quoting a bunch of nonsense to make myself feel better.

When you write down specific memories, you give context and real examples to your affirmations. It's powerful, and I can only say that you should try this if you haven't already. Or, if you have done it, and have neglected this task, you may need to pick the habit up again. Especially if you've been struggling to feel valuable.

CONCLUSION

As for now, we should conclude with some of the key points we have discussed. They are:

1. Self worth is intrinsic. It's something that's in us, whether we know it or not, or whether or not we think we deserve it.

2. Self-worth differs from self-esteem. Self-esteem pertains to how we see ourselves. It can change depending on how we feel. Self-worth refers to something that cannot change, no matter what we are feeling.

3. Our inability to sense our own self-worth is often the root problem from which many of our other problems spring up, such as timidity, loneliness, complacency in life, and much more.

4. It's hard for us to believe what the Scriptures tell us about our value. And, we tend to easily believe our own negative self-talk. We derive our own self-perspectives from others and their perspectives of us.

5. We use the world's yardstick to measure each other and ourselves. But, it doesn't work because our worth isn't calculated by adding up our actions and our accomplishments. We are valuable, not because of what we've done, but because of who we are – children of the Most High God.

6. What's needed more than knowledge is faith. Faith that I'm making progress and that my efforts are making a difference. If I can believe this, it means I really am getting closer to understanding God's love (as well as my own value).

7. If you were once a child, then you have a reference point – for who you are, and who you may have drifted away from. And, like an old home, your best improvements will probably involve stripping things away, rather than adding. Allow the love and acceptance of good people to chip away at those cold, hard parts of you that you've used to protect yourself and disguise yourself with.

8. As you walk through the busy streets of life, remember to pause and play. Let your worth shine. Play your heart out, even if no one stops to listen. It's not a reflection of your worth. After all, it's not really them you're playing for. It's not them you're really trying to please. More than anyone else, you crave the acceptance of yourself. Your reason for letting yourself shine has nothing to do with the recognition that it may bring. It has to do with the fact

that God gave you strength and purpose, and it would be a shame to keep them hidden.

9. Keep a few good people nearby who will always remind you that you matter, even when no one else is saying so. You can let the love of others in, even though you're not depending on them for confirmation of your value.

10. Write down the good truths about you. Good memories. Good moments. Write down the good things others have seen in you. Keep these things in view. Try hard not to forget that God is smiling down on you, glad that He made you. Happy when you are happy. Hurt when you feel hurt. Wanting you to know that you are loved. You are cherished. You… have value.

THE END

A PERSONAL NOTE TO THE READER

Dear Reader,

I would like to offer my heartfelt thanks to you for reading this book, and I would also like to let you know how much I depend on you. I am at your mercy. My fate as a writer depends largely upon how much value you have received from my work, and upon how compelled you feel to continue reading it, and spreading your knowledge of it to those you know. Without your help, I will almost certainly never have the impact I dream of having, or affect the number of lives I hope to affect.

This is why I ask you now, dear reader, to take a moment and reflect upon what you have just read. How has it impacted you? Were you challenged? Awakened? Or what about encouraged? If so, then I would only ask you to be faithful – not to me, but to your own feelings of inspiration, and to spread the sunlight you've experienced into the lives of those you know who may need it.

If you can think of anyone who may benefit by this book, then please send them a quick text or email, or give them a phone call. Shoot them the link in a Facebook message, if that's your thing. Tell them about this encouraging, undiscovered book that you know would shed light on their lives.

To me, it is unimportant whether or not I make another sale. What's important is that your encouragement doesn't end with you but that the fire that has been kindled keeps spreading. I honestly don't care whether they purchase the book, borrow it, or find a free copy of it floating around in a library. What matters to me is that the message is passed along. And oh yeah… that it is applied.

Thank you, once again.

Sincerely,

C J Kruse

ALL BOOKS BY CJ KRUSE

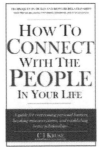

Made in the USA
Las Vegas, NV
09 November 2021